"I have found the book, *Overc[...]* Shirley Babior and Carol Gold[...] short-term treatment of patient[...] disorders. The descriptive passag[...]

thoughts' to 'rational responses' seems to immediately illuminate the cognitive process for most panic responders. They are then able to identify the irrational thinking quickly, as it occurs. This, in conjunction with the many other techniques described in the book, provides an excellent basis for continued self-help procedure."

John E. D[...]
Clinical [...]
Departm[...]
The Mary Imogene Bassett Hospital
Affiliate of Columbia University

"My number one resource for symptom reduction—comprehensive yet succinct—an invaluable daily reference for long-term recovery of all anxiety disorders."

Julie Britz, MSW, LICSW
Psychotherapist
Harvard Community Health Plan

"Babior and Goldman have written a book that is quite valuable for the very many patients who ask the treating physician for guidance in contributing to their own treatment. The book has no jargon, advances no theoretical claims, avoids the usual disparaging remarks about medical treatments, and makes no unrealistic promises. "This book will certainly help the very many patients who want to take an active role in their own treatment."

Rodrigo A. Munoz, M.D., F.A.P.A.
Clinical Professor of Psychiatry
University of California, San Diego
Book Review Editor
Annals of Clinical Psychiatry
3200 Fourth Avenue, Suite 204
San Diego, California 92103

A PROGRAM FOR RECOVERY

Overcoming
PANIC
ATTACKS

Strategies to Free Yourself from the Anxiety Trap

Shirley Babior, LCSW, MFCC
Carol Goldman, LICSW

Whole Person Associates
Pfeifer-Hamilton Publishers
Duluth, Minnesota

Whole Person Associates
Pfeifer-Hamilton Publishers
210 West Michigan
Duluth MN 55802-1908   218-727-0500

Overcoming Panic Attacks

Printed in the United States of America by Banta

10   9   8   7   6   5   4   3   2   1

Library of Congress Cataloging in Publication Data
    Babior, Shirley, 1938–
        Overcoming panic attacks: strategies to free yourself from the
    anxiety trap/by Shirley Babior, Carol Goldman.
            p.   cm.
        ISBN 1-57025-045-6
        1. Panic attacks. 2. Relaxation. 3. Panic attacks—Case studies.
    4. Self-care, Health. I. Goldman, Carol, 1950–   . II. Title.
    RC535.B24 1991
    616.85'223—dc20   90-46074
                                                                      CIP

Cover and interior design by Lillian Svec
Illustrations by J. Whiting and Thayne Wickam

Inquiries, orders, and catalog requests should be addressed to
Whole Person Associates
210 West Michigan
Duluth Minnesota 55802-1908
800-247-6789

The instructions and advice discussed in this book are in no way intended as a substitute for medical or psychological counseling. Consult a professional before determining the nature of your problem. The authors and the publisher disclaim any responsibility or liability resulting from the application of procedures advocated or discussed in this book.

All personal accounts of recovery are used with permission. Names have been changed to protect their anonymity.

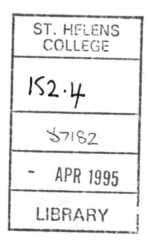

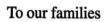

To our families

Acknowledgments

We are indebted to the pioneering work of Aaron Beck, Herbert Benson, David Clark, David Barlow, Andrew Mathews, Michael Gelder, Derek Johnston, Diane Chambless, Alan Goldstein, Isaac Marks, and Claire Weekes.

CONTENTS

3 How Family and Friends Can Help
Do's and Don't's for Those Who Care

4 It Feels So Good to Feel Good Again!
Personal Stories of Recovery

   • Ten men and women tell how they overcame
     panic attacks in their lives

EXPOSURE STRATEGY LIST

FIRST ALERT CARDS

Introduction

During the past twelve years we have treated many clients with panic attacks and other anxiety disorders as part of our clinical practice. It has been a very satisfying field in which to do psychotherapy. Our clients are usually very conscientious and relieved to be working with someone who understands their problem. In addition, treatment itself has progressed to a point where we can be confident that relief is usually possible. It has been very rewarding for us to help our clients overcome their panic and avoidance reactions through the individualized application of appropriate therapy. We have experienced the pleasure of accompanying clients on elevators, in shopping malls, in supermarkets, or while flying, as they achieve success — perhaps after many years of avoidance or "white-knuckling." It has been equally gratifying to watch a person's confidence grow as he or she recovers and begins to interact with the world more assertively.

We have been professional friends and colleagues for many years. In 1985, we founded the Greater Boston Phobia Society, an organization composed of psychotherapists, and people with phobias and their families. This society organizes forums to educate the public about treatment options, publishes a newsletter, maintains a treatment referral list, and helps form support groups.

A few years ago, we decided to write a handbook for people with panic attacks, as well as their families and their therapists, to use as a key part of their recovery program. We wanted this book to include the latest research, yet be small enough to carry easily and consult as often as needed.

In the middle of the project, one of us moved to San Diego, which has led to long hours on the telephone and repeated visits to the Federal Express office in order to finish what we had begun. Looking back on the process, however, we are more than pleased to finally be able to offer this guide to those suffering from panic and to others who are close to them.

We encourage people suffering from panic attacks and phobic avoidance to seek individual, medical, and psychological assessment, so that all factors contributing to the problem can be identified and treated. We hope the suggestions for seeking professional help at the end of the booklet may prove helpful.

We wish you success on your path to recovery, and are delighted that you are taking this book with you on your journey. We hope it helps. And we welcome your comments and suggestions.

Shirley Babior
Carol Goldman

1

How to Cope with Panic Attacks

Strategies to Free Yourself from the Anxiety Trap

Panic attacks are terrifying experiences that seem to strike from nowhere! The sensations can be very sudden and so extreme you think your life is in danger! The feelings are so painful that you dread, maybe more than anything else, having to go through that again. So, you may find yourself on guard every waking moment, scanning situations for danger, so you won't be caught by another surprise attack. The idea of being trapped by a paralyzing, painful fear is almost too much to handle. Are you dying? Or worse yet, are you crazy? Who can you confide in? What on earth can you do? Are you the only one who feels this way?

Actually, by now you've probably heard about panic attacks, or anxiety attacks, and you may already know that they impair the quality of life for over a million people. These attacks are the physical sensations of extreme fear, triggered by an anxious or panicky thought, occurring when the fear reaction is inappropriate because there's no real danger present. However, after you've had this very unpleasant experience, even the slightest physical sensation of anxiety can set off the reaction again, stimulating your automatic nervous system and beginning an ever-increasing cycle of panic, stress, and fear.

These attacks are exhausting, discouraging, and can be very depressing. However, there is some very good news for you!

You *can* overcome panic attacks.
You *can* be free of the pain.

And life can return to normal again — or maybe even be better than it was before!

Panic attacks happen as the result of responses you learned without being aware of what you were doing. Therefore, what you have to do, as thousands of others have done, is un-learn or dismantle this reaction. You can do this by understanding what is really happening to you and then by practicing the techniques you'll read about in this book. First, though, let's discuss what not to do.

In a desperate attempt to prevent further attacks, many people respond by:

- Avoiding all situations where panic attacks might occur, where help isn't available, or where they feel unsafe.
- Becoming preoccupied with the next attack, monitoring their own internal sensations for signals that an attack is imminent.

Unfortunately, these reactions often lead to greater fear and as fear intensifies and avoidance increases, the problem gets worse.

How can we reverse this debilitating process? Since there are two aspects to the problem — fear of panic attacks and subsequent avoidance of situations where they might occur — the solution involves two components:

1. Reducing the fear of panic attacks, while dealing with internal sensations of anxiety.
2. Ending avoidance of panic-associated situations and panic-associated sensations.

The first step on the road to recovery is understanding that **a panic attack is not dangerous.** The second step involves work: **you have to face panic-associated situations and cope with whatever feelings you have.** Fortunately, there are appropriate ways to approach these situations, and many concrete strategies to help you succeed. We will cover each of these topics step by step, to prepare you to challenge and then conquer your problem. As therapists, we have witnessed change in a great many people. We have written this book so you, too, can recover.

This book is full of strategies and techniques for overcoming anxiety. You can personalize the messages by creating your own **First Alert Cards.** At the back of the book there are cards you can clip out, or you can use 3" x 5" file cards, if you prefer, and fill them with statements or cue words that are meaningful to you — the key ideas you want to remember. Keep these cards with you as long as you need them. Take them out to read when you are anxious or in a panic situation. Refer to them at different points in your recovery for instant guidance and support. Read them when you are relaxed and you'll realize how much progress you've made and how far you've come.

You may wish to read through this chapter once in order to get a general idea of what it is all about. There are two very important forms at the end of the chapter for you to fill out, "My Targets for Change Checklist" and "My Anxiety Rating Scale." Then you can go back over the material to work on your individual problems and plan how to deal with them.

THE WHYS AND WHERES OF PANIC ATTACKS

Picture the way your body reacts when you are in real danger — in a fire, for example. Your heart starts beating more rapidly, your stomach may tense, you sweat and shake. You have activated the "fight or flight response" which prepares you to battle or to flee from danger. With panic attacks these same reactions occur, but they are triggered even though there is no real danger — they are false alarms. We can't always discover why this process begins, but typically it starts after an illness, a pregnancy, a drug experience, relationship problems, loss of a loved one, moving your home, or a period of prolonged tension. After this "false alarm" reaction occurs a few times, it may begin to recur in specific situations. The reason this happens is that the site of a former panic attack becomes scary by association.

Let's explore this process in detail. If you had a recent panic attack in a supermarket and your dominant sensation was a racing heart, just thinking of going back to the supermarket can raise your anxiety level and cause your heart to race. **It is not really the market you fear — it's the likelihood of your having a panic attack while you are there!**

You feel vulnerable because of your past experience. However, it's crucial to understand that what you really have developed is a fear of your own sensations of panic, not of the place itself. This is so important that you may want to write it down on your First Alert Card so you'll have a concrete reminder as you work to overcome this problem.

Some of the common places associated with panic are crowded places, such as stores, churches, theaters, subways, buses, and restaurants. Panic can come up almost anywhere you feel trapped — at the dentist, a social situation, waiting in a line, in a class, on bridges, in tunnels, cars, sometimes just being at home. The intensity of your fear may vary from day to day, causing you to wonder about your sanity, and creating fluctuations in your ability to face or avoid the situations you dread. Sometimes you can only face these situations with a trusted companion.

For most panic sufferers, the intervals between panic attacks are consumed with worry about what might happen (the "what if..." kind of thinking), because it is never easy to tell when the next panic attack may come. Thoughts about the next "surprise attack" are never far away! This "anticipatory" anxiety may become worse as you begin to constantly monitor the physical or mental sensations you associate with panic. In fact, for some people, the anxiety caused by the anticipation of panic is much worse than the anxiety they actually feel in a panic-associated situation. Anticipatory anxiety can lead to years of avoidance behavior, even when actual panic attacks are not occurring or happen only occasionally. In some cases, anticipatory thinking keeps the fear alive by creating anxiety about how you think you *might* feel in the future.

You may also begin to become fearful of all kinds of sensations and activities you previously experienced as normal. Suddenly, physical sensations associated with exercise, sex, or watching exciting movies may cause these activities to become frightening. This hypervigilance can occur anytime you misinterpret harmless excitement as a predictor of panic.

If you are experiencing panic attacks, a thorough medical examination is essential in order to rule out an underlying physical disorder. If you have an examination and are told you are in good health, it's time to learn to deal with your panic attacks in a new way.

WHAT IS HAPPENING TO ME?

To understand panic attacks, let's look at the way panic affects you. There are three separate levels: physiological (your physical feelings), cognitive (your thoughts), and behavioral (your actions).

The **physical feelings** of a panic attack vary from person to person, but common symptoms are heart palpitations, chest pain or discomfort, choking or smothering sensations, dizziness, tingling in your hands or feet, feelings of unreality or disorientation, sweating, faintness, trembling, or shortness of breath.

In your case, one symptom — shortness of breath, for example — might be the strongest and most troublesome, and this single sensation, associated with fear, can trigger your panic. In this case, you might begin to monitor your breathing in certain situations, trying to detect the slightest change. Any perceived change in breathing, even when a change is due entirely to a benign cause such as exercise, can trigger fear which can lead to a panic attack. When the initial, mild signs of anxiety, exertion, or excitement no longer frighten you, you will be well on your way to recovery.

Now, let's look at your **thoughts** and how they influence your feelings. Panic attacks occur suddenly and can be very intense. The physical sensations are accompanied by fearful thoughts. Because there doesn't seem to be any reasonable explanation for what you're feeling, your thoughts may turn to various kinds of catastrophes that could possibly happen in the future. You may think, "I might have a heart attack, hurt myself or others, faint, scream, jump out of the car, or lose all control and go crazy." These thoughts naturally aggravate the fear and can actually make the physical symptoms worse, as well as convince you that something terrible is about to happen.

So, a cycle begins: the physical symptoms are followed by fear, which leads to catastrophic thoughts, which leads to greater fear, which leads to more marked physical symptoms, and so on. You may already realize that your thoughts are alarming you and making your anxiety worse. However, what many people don't realize is that what they've become so terrified of is their own physical sensations, and so they try to avoid them in order to stay calm and in control. It is certainly true that these sensations are distressing, but it is just as true, as we said earlier, that through understanding and practice, you can bring this episode of your life to an end, *no matter how long you've suffered!*

Regarding your **actions**, panicky feelings give rise to an instinct to flee from the situation and escape to a safer place. This can lead to a hasty departure! If you feel less anxious when you escape, you strengthen your impulse to escape when you are in a similar situation again. Escape reinforces your faulty logic that your panic is connected to place. (More about this later.)

A second kind of avoidance involves trying to escape from your physical sensations by distraction. Trying not to feel those things associated with the onset of panic, you may pretend to be elsewhere, or perform repetitious tasks unrelated to the situation in order to block these feelings. You may fight to stay completely in control by "white-knuckling," tensing, and catastrophizing all the while. These strategies can cause you to believe that these unpleasant, but harmless sensations are dangerous, but this is simply not true. While these strategies may allow you to carry on with your routine, they may reinforce your fears. On later pages we will acquaint you with coping techniques designed to lower your panic level while you remain focused on your usual routine.

Although there is no single treatment that works for everyone, there is one essential ingredient in overcoming panic and that is exposure to the places and the physical sensations you now associate with panic. (You didn't always feel this way, remember?) Also, since probably your greatest fear is of how bad you'll feel, it is essential that you reduce your fear of the anxiety attacks themselves, by learning new ways to cope with anxiety — using some simple skills and lots of hard work.

Remember: you have a greater capacity to influence your level of anxiety than you think!

A New Attitude about Anxiety

People who suffer from panic attacks have a problem, but not the problem they think they have. So, in your case, you may think you are dying, going crazy, or losing control. However, mistaking these symptoms of anxiety for the signs of imminent disaster only makes the symptoms more severe.

A new attitude means *facing up to anxiety and panic instead of avoiding them.* There are many techniques that can help put this new attitude into practice. These can involve:

- Techniques to address physical symptoms;
- Cognitive techniques for thought change; and
- Behavioral plans to alter escape and avoidance behavior.

Let's look at each group in turn.

PRACTICING NEW WAYS TO RELAX

Techniques for Reducing the Physical Symptoms of Anxiety

If you have panic attacks, you are probably experiencing a lot of tension in your life. You may feel wound up or pressured, and probably for very important reasons. This high

level of anxiety can cause you to overreact to stressful situations. For this reason, we are including descriptions of
simple techniques you can use to help reduce this general
level of tension. Try them all to see which works best.
When you find one that works particularly well for you,
write it down on your First Alert Card, so you can read it
when you may be too anxious to remember it.

Many of the symptoms you're experiencing are really
aspects of the way you are breathing, called hyperventila-
tion. Feeling slightly nervous, you begin to breathe
shallowly, faster than usual, in short, choppy breaths or
forced breaths, all of which tends to increase the severity
of the symptoms.

For many people, it's extremely helpful to **practice
even, slow, gentle breathing** before and during a stressful situation. One way to be sure you are breathing this
way is to take a slow, gentle breath through your nose, hold
it for a second, and then slowly breathe out through your
mouth, pursing your lips as if you're sipping through a
straw. Try inhaling to the count of eight, pausing, and
exhaling to a count of eight.

You can also try putting your hand on your stomach.
If you are breathing properly, slowly, and from your
diaphragm, you should be able to see your hand rise and
fall as you inhale and exhale. If you continue breathing
in this slow, deliberate way, often you will notice that your
symptoms will be less severe, and your level of anxiety
will lower dramatically.

You might also try to **think of a cue word that is
calming to you**, such as the word *calm* itself, or the word
relax, or *peace*. Often it helps to say the calming cue word
to yourself each time you slowly exhale. This will help

you concentrate on the physical sensations of relaxation, allowing yourself to become calmer and more in control.

Practice these breathing techniques two or three times each day during calm intervals for a few weeks. After practicing during uneventful times, begin to use these breathing techniques as coping strategies during panic.

Another technique, which combines slow breathing techniques with imagery, is to imagine that you are lying on a beach, feeling the warm sun shining from above and the warm sand beneath you. Center your breathing in your diaphragm, repeating "warm" on the in-breath and "release" on the out-breath while you switch off your muscles, letting the tension go. Sun and sand work well in this exercise, but any images you find relaxing will work. For example, if you don't live near the coast, maybe for you, the relaxing image is lying on a picnic blanket on the lawn in the warm sun. Use whatever image is meaningful to release your tension.

Other techniques can also be effective in helping you learn to relax when you experience a great deal of tension in your body. Even though you have nothing to fear, it's very likely that you are holding your muscles tightly, as if you had to prepare for a disaster. It's possible that you've never really learned to relax. If that is the case, learning to relax can help with panic attacks, because your body will be less stressed and you can practice physically letting go of tension when you begin to feel low levels of anxiety. After you practice, fill out the "Tension/Relaxation Rating Sheet" on page 47 before and after each relaxation session.

If you are experiencing anxiety rather than relaxation while doing these exercises, then you gain an opportunity to feel these physical sensations and interpret them as harmless. Throughout the program in this book, you will be learning that **false alarms of danger are opportunities to practice** what you're learning. For example, you can de-catastrophize; that is, you can learn to think about what is really happening at the moment, instead of worrying about what horrible tragedy could possibly occur.

One technique that is often useful is called progressive muscle relaxation. Make yourself comfortable, in a chair or lying down, and then begin to tighten and relax specific muscles in your body. First, slowly tense those particular muscles as much as you can, stopping short of causing cramping or pain, and then notice the feeling in the tight muscles. Next, suddenly release the tension and enjoy the pleasant feeling of relaxation. Study the contrast between the tension and the relaxation in each area of your body as you go along. While you are practicing, try to hold the muscles tense for at least five seconds and relax for at least thirty seconds. Some parts of your body — your back, for example, which has many more muscles than other parts — may require more time. If you still feel tension in a certain area of your muscles after you finish tensing and relaxing it, you may choose to repeat the exercise before moving on.

Here are more exercises for you to try:

1. Wrinkle your forehead, noticing the tension at the bridge of your nose and over each eyebrow. Now release the tension and feel it slowly ease away.
2. Wrinkle your nose and notice the tension at the bridge and nostrils. Pay special attention to the areas that are particularly tense. Now relax and notice how the muscles feel.

3. Close your eyes tightly. Now relax your eyes as you release the tension and notice the difference in how you feel.

4. Make yourself smile as widely as you can. Your lips and cheeks should feel tense. Now relax the muscles in your cheeks, and notice how they feel. Focus on the sensations of increasing relaxation and concentrate on enjoying it.

5. Clench your teeth as hard as you can without causing pain. Now relax your jaw, and think about enjoying the sensation of letting go.

6. Tighten your neck. Pay special attention to the areas where you feel tension, especially the back and sides of your neck. Now let go as much as you possibly can. Then let go a little more.

7. Make a fist in front of you, holding your arm out straight, and make your entire arm as rigid as you can. Notice how tense it is. Now relax and lower your arm, allowing your hand to hang naturally at your side. Again, notice how different it feels.

8. Raise your leg. Turn your toes up and back and make the whole leg rigid. Now slowly relax and lower your leg, letting your toes go. Again, notice how different it feels.

9. Bring your fists up high on your chest, pull them back and clench them as hard as you can. Notice how your shoulders and back feel. Now slowly open your hands and let your arms fall, noticing the difference.

10. While sitting down, tighten all the muscles below your waist as hard as you can. You should feel yourself rise off the chair a little. Notice where

the tension is, especially the tops and bottoms of your thighs. Now gently relax all your leg muscles, and notice how relaxed you feel.

Repeat this sequence of exercises as often as you can. After a while, you can practice relaxing just that certain part of your body that feels tense. Eventually you should be able to relax without the tense-and-release regime, particularly if you also practice slow, relaxed breathing.

The common goal of using any of these exercises is to produce a feeling of physical well-being. Another way to achieve this is to practice the "relaxation response," as taught by Dr. Herbert Benson in his book, *The Relaxation Response.* If you sit comfortably, relaxing your body into the chair, taking slow, natural breaths and repeating a word or phrase for ten to twenty minutes daily, you can experience the powerful impact of this response. If, during this time, other thoughts arise, don't worry. Just return to your key word. If you follow these instructions, the relaxation response will occur automatically. For anxiety sufferers, the feeling of calm will be very beneficial throughout the rest of the day.

Scripts

Scripts are another device to use for relaxation, so that you have a familiar voice reminding you how to relax. Here are three short scripts that you or a friend can record. When you need to relax, try playing the tape back. This can be in your car, if you like. Sometimes it is helpful just to listen to the tape, even if you cannot do the exercises. Focusing on the instructions will allow you to replace your inaccurate, scary thoughts with accurate, coping affirmations.

Script 1

Make yourself comfortable. Close your eyes if appropriate. Now stretch your legs as far as you can, turn your toes back and tighten all the muscles in your feet as tightly as you can. Hold it . . . . Now tighten all the muscles in your calves and thighs. Make each leg as rigid as possible, and hold it . . . hold it . . . . Now let your legs go completely limp and feel the relaxation in every part of your leg, in your toes, your feet, your thighs. It's a wonderful feeling.

Now, stretch out your hands and make a fist. Make it tight, tighter, tighter . . . and hold it. Now make your arms rigid, and feel the muscles in your forearm and biceps. Hold it. Hold it. Good. Now relax, all the way. Let your arms hang limp, and notice how loose they feel, how relaxed, how wonderful.

Now arch your back, and tighten every muscle you can find in your back and neck. Make a face, as tight as you can, and hold it, hold everything . . . keep holding . . . keep holding . . . . Now I am going to count backwards from 10, and as I do, I want you to think of a scene that makes you feel very calm, very relaxed, and while I am counting and you are thinking about that, I want you to slowly relax all those tense muscles. I am counting down, now, 10, 9, 8, 7, let it go, slowly, 6, 5, 4, 3, 2, 1. Good. Now you are completely relaxed, free of tension in your body, and you can feel the wellness spreading throughout inside you, and on your face, and in your legs and shoulders. Good. Now just enjoy that wonderful feeling of relaxation. Soon you will open your eyes if they are closed. Good. All right, open your eyes. You feel wonderfully well and very relaxed.

Script 2

I may be frightened now. I may feel like running away. But stop! Listen! *Everything will be fine.* What I feel now will go away with time. This will pass . . . . Nothing terrible will happen. I ask myself, "What is actually happening at this moment?" I notice the sensations in my body. They cannot harm me. I am safe, because what I am afraid of is something that won't really happen. It never has and it never will, because my body will take care of itself.

Take a gentle, slow breath. Inhale slowly and evenly. Hold it . . . and exhale, slowly, slowly. My body can do this. Try it again — inhale, slowly . . . hold it . . . exhale, very slowly. While I exhale, I will let myself slump wherever I am, just letting all my muscles relax, like I am a rag doll . . . . Good. I will let my shoulders hang down.

I know how much those scary thoughts have controlled my life. It is unfair that they should have that much control over me. I am going to replace those thoughts with some more rational ones. I can complete what I set out to do, because this fear will pass. *It will pass.*

Now take another slow, gentle breath . . . hold it . . . and let it go, very slowly. I will let my muscles go as I exhale, slowly. I will not worry if I become more aware of my fear. . . . It will go away.

I will think about what is happening right this very minute. Where am I? What am I doing? What is actually going on at this very moment? No matter how convinced I am that something terrible is going to happen this very minute, it will not.

I am doing something very hard. I am choosing to feel these physical sensations now so that I can feel better tomorrow. I am being very brave, in a new way . . . these feelings will not harm me, I am safe. Panic has never harmed anyone. This is a difficult thing to realize, but eventually the panic will fade as I continue to practice my coping techniques.

I will try another slow, gentle breath through my nose. Inhale . . . hold it . . . and exhale, very slowly, letting my muscles go while I exhale. Good.

I won't let these scary thoughts and feelings run my life. I will decide. I will choose to continue with what I am doing right now. I may feel more discomfort now, but on the other side of that discomfort is greater self-confidence and a better life. I am safe and I will feel better. The more I practice dealing with these scary feelings, the better I will be at mastering them.

Script 3

Take a slow, gentle breath and say to yourself, "Calm and relax. Just relax." Relax more and more. Feel the relaxation in your forehead. Your forehead muscles are becoming loose, limp, and heavy. Just feel the eyelids relaxing. Allow your cheek and jaw muscles to relax more and more. Feel the relaxation in your neck and your shoulders and just allow all the tension to leave your arms and your fingertips. Take another slow, gentle breath and as you exhale, say to yourself, "Calm and relaxed."

Feel the relaxation going into your chest and your stomach and your hips and your legs as you allow your body to relax more and more. Just let the tension go and feel your feet and toes relaxing more and more. Take another slow, gentle breath and say to yourself, "It feels really good to be calm, peaceful, and relaxed." Continue to relax your body as long as you wish, allowing all the muscles to relax more and more. Just allow the tension to switch off. Take another slow, gentle breath and say to yourself, "Calm and relaxed."

While you are doing this exercise, you might want to put some pleasurable, soothing music on in the background and close your eyes if you feel comfortable doing so. Or if you prefer, keep your eyes open. That's fine too. Make yourself as comfortable as possible. Take in a slow, gentle breath. Exhale and feel even more of the tension leaving. Continue your slow, gentle breathing. With every inhale, relax further and further. With every exhale, let a little more of the tension leave your body. Let the tension go wherever it wants to go. Just imagine your muscles relaxing more and more.

Continue to breathe slowly and gently. Think about the journey you are going to be taking on your way to recovery. As with any journey, you must first make the decision to go. Pick an image that is particularly comforting to you for your personal journey. Imagine going on water or in the woods or on a peaceful path. Perhaps the journey will feel most comforting if it is just a relaxing walk through your own house.

Unexpected things will sometimes occur on your journey to recovery. You're going to get all kinds of information in this book that will help when you hit a trouble spot. You will be prepared for these possibilities.

Take some time to think about the information you've gotten in this book up to now. Don't worry about learning the material. The learning is already taking place. Continue to read the book and think about your own recovery. You'll be reading about coping strategies that will be useful as you move forward on your journey — strategies that will help you overcome your own particular roadblocks. Maybe there are one or two ideas you've read about before that have meaning for you but you haven't learned how to use yet or perhaps the most useful strategies are brand new. Now that you've begun the journey to recovery, continue to move forward and begin to focus on the satisfactions that await you, as you feel better and better.

● ● ●

After reading each chapter in this book, turn to the exercises in this chapter and use them again. Keep focused on the points that will have the most impact for you as you continue on your journey — the journey from panic to recovery. Each time you do an exercise, take a moment to silently (or aloud) repeat these points, these comments, to fix them in your mind. Write them down on your First Alert Card now.

Rating Your Feelings of Panic

Think of your feelings of panic on a scale of 0 to 10, where 0 is totally relaxed and 10 is the very worst feeling of panic you've ever experienced. Doing this, you will begin to differentiate between your own levels of anxiety. We've included a form at the end of this chapter to help you. Now, for any anxiety you feel, you can assign a number on this scale.

Rating your own anxiety level is very helpful so that you won't always anticipate the worst possible attack. When you are aware that you feel lower levels of anxiety, as well as the high one, it becomes a kind of cue to remind you before your anxiety spirals upwards. You will have time to respond to mild anxiety in ways that can calm you instead of alarm you. For example, as you enter a shopping mall you experience mild (level 3, for example) heart palpitations or a slight feeling of shakiness. You may begin to take short, shallow breaths, which will exaggerate your symptoms. However, remembering that a less anxious response is possible, you will have time to slow down and begin using some of the relaxation methods that you've learned. Any relaxation method, like those outlined above, can dramatically reduce these symptoms and help avert a panic attack.

When you feel extreme panic and may be feeling very disoriented, you can try one of the coping techniques, such as slow, gentle, deep breathing to lower your anxiety level. You may or may not succeed. But if your anxiety level remains high, do not fight to control it — let it happen. Let the feelings run their course. **Remind yourself that there is nothing to fear.** Observe your symptoms. You may even decide to make one symptom feel worse, like making your heart, which is already beating fast, beat even faster. **Notice that catastrophes do not occur, though, even when you** *try* **to bring them on.**

If you are having difficulty focusing on using these techniques due to extreme and frequent panic, evaluation for medication by a doctor who specializes in anxiety medication may be indicated. On the other hand, you might want to give yourself more time to adapt to these new ways of dealing with your physical sensations. Discuss these options with your therapist and with your doctor.

If you are already on an anti-panic medication or decide to start one at this time, still proceed with the suggestions outlined in this handbook in order to overcome your anticipatory fears and deal with those situations you avoid.

HOW CAN I CHANGE MY THINKING?

Cognitive Techniques for Overcoming Anxiety

As you begin to observe your levels of fear (on the 0 to 10 scale), you will notice that those levels are not constant. Your anxiety, in fact, goes up and down. You may begin to notice that the fear goes up when you are concentrating more on your most frightening thoughts and bodily reactions.

It would be helpful to notice your level of panic, and also listen carefully to the messages you are sending yourself about your symptoms. It may be very normal to have some level of tension in certain situations, like having to give a speech or getting on an airplane. However, the difference between feeling an anxiety level of 1 or 2 in some situations and a level 10 in others can be the result of your own thoughts. If you predict that a catastrophe will occur, or that you will be unable to cope, or that you will need to escape, your fearful feelings will intensify. Catastrophic thinking causes people with panic attacks to misinterpret anxiety symptoms as being dangerous.

Fortunately, there is another more rational voice always with you. By focusing on this reassuring voice, you can bring a level of 10 back down. We call this voice the "Rational You." The Rational You "thinks" its way through life's events evaluating the degrees of safety versus danger involved. It can reassure and comfort you when you are okay. What happens to this part of you in panic situations? It gets pushed aside when you focus on the anxiety sensations and misinterpret them as dangerous.

In order to strengthen the Rational You, examine the specific thoughts that increase your feelings of panic and deliberately try to develop alternate ways of thinking. This is called rational responding, or de-catastrophizing.

For example, the thought, "I am going crazy" might be replaced with, "I am just experiencing physical symptoms. I have no reason to think I'm going crazy." "I'm going to faint" could be replaced with, "I've never fainted before and there is no evidence that I'm going to now." Adding those soothing words and phrases that you have developed, such as "relax," "it will pass," "it's just my heart beating — I'm not dying," as well as slow, gentle breathing exercises will also help.

Carry your First Alert Card with your catastrophic predictions on one side and your rational responses on the other. Before entering a situation where you think panic might occur, read the card and focus on the rational response. When you are plagued with catastrophic thoughts, talk to yourself as objectively as you can. Do you have any evidence to support those thoughts that disaster might happen? Is there any other way you could view the situation? This exercise will usually allow you to see that you have been concentrating on the worst possible, but by no means the most likely, outcome.

You can also try what is called "here and now" focusing. Allow your awareness of panicky thoughts to recede and, instead, concentrate intently on what is around you. Pay attention to the colors, sights, smells, sounds, and tasks at hand. When panic thoughts intrude, use them as reminders to refocus your attention on the actual situation. Stay focused on what you are feeling now — "I feel my heart beating," for example, rather than "I am going to have a heart attack." Stay attuned to the situation, rather than to your fear of what may be about to happen.

People who develop extreme fear reactions sometimes label every feeling they have as anxiety. This is another error in logic or judgment. See if you can identify feelings other than fear or anxiety when you are experiencing discomfort. Perhaps you're excited, sad, lonely, angry, or disappointed. Ask yourself, "What would I be feeling right now if I weren't feeling anxious?"

Another way to say this is, "What else am I feeling underneath my fear?" If those other uncomfortable feelings are due to something other than anxiety, you may be able to work on solving the other problems or accepting some of those feelings as normal parts of being alive.

CATASTROPHIC THOUGHTS AND
RATIONAL RESPONSES

1. Catastrophic thought: "I always panic when ...."
   Rational response: "I don't always have a panic attack, even when I worry about 'what ifs.'"

2. Catastrophic thought: "Suppose I faint?"
   Rational response: "I've never before fainted from panic."

3. Catastrophic thought: "What if I have a panic attack?"
   Rational response: "If I do panic, I can tolerate the pain again, just like I have before."

4. Catastrophic thought: "What if I have to leave and ruin someone else's good time?"
   Rational response: "I probably won't have to leave, but if I do, people will understand and be supportive."

5. Catastrophic thought: "I know I'll have a heart attack or stroke."
   Rational response: "The physical symptoms of anxiety are not dangerous. My body is merely reacting to my fears."

6. Catastrophic thought: "I might die!"
   Rational response: "No one has ever died from a panic attack."

7. Catastrophic thought: "I'll lose control and make a fool of myself."
   Rational response: "I may get confused when I'm anxious, but I don't lose control."

8. Catastrophic thought: "I'll be trapped!"
   Rational response: "I have options."

9. Catastrophic thought: "People will notice how embarrassed I am!"
   Rational response: "So what if people notice how embarrassed I am? Most people won't notice, and those who do may be understanding and helpful."

10. Catastrophic thought: "I'll be so embarrassed if I hyperventilate."
    Rational response: "If I hyperventilate, I'll remember to take slow, gentle breaths."

11. Catastrophic thought: "I'm sure I'll go crazy."
    Rational response: "I'm not crazy — I'm nervous or anxious. There's a big difference between being anxious and crazy."

Differentiating anxiety from fatigue, hunger, or your physical response to caffeine, heat, or humidity can reduce the potential of panic attacks. (This is called reattribution.) Some people are afraid to feel intense emotion and get anxious if they are very sad, angry, etc. The more you begin to identify and get comfortable with your entire range of emotions, the less scary and more manageable all your emotions will become.

How long have you had this fear of heights?

Many of our irrational thoughts spring from basic beliefs about ourselves, especially, and about others as well. These beliefs usually come from childhood and are very deeply ingrained. If unexamined, these beliefs may cause you to dismiss or discount the Rational You.

Here are some common basic assumptions which are associated with anxiety problems. Are any of these assumptions getting in your way?

Perfectionism

- Do you feel a constant pressure to achieve?
- Do you criticize yourself when you aren't perfect?
- Do you feel you haven't done enough no matter how hard you try?
- Do you give up pleasure in order to be the best at everything you do?

Control

- Do you have to be perfectly in control at all times?
- Do you worry about how you appear to others when you are anxious?
- Do you feel that any lack of control is a sign of weakness or failure?
- Can you feel safe if you allow someone else to take over control of a situation?

People-pleasing

- Does your self-esteem depend on everyone else's opinion of you?
- Do you feel unable to manage on your own?
- Are you better at caring for others than caring for yourself?
- Do you keep feelings of anger inside to avoid displeasing others?

If you answered yes to some of these statements, it is possible that these beliefs have become roadblocks to your recovery. For example, if you believe, "I have to be perfectly calm at all times," you may be adding unnecessary tension to everyday life. **No one is calm all the time!** However, this thought adds tension and makes you more vulnerable to panic. Be aware that these beliefs are really a strong part of you.

The first step to changing these beliefs is to notice the impact they have on your anxiety level. After you do that, you then have choices. You can try different experiments. For example, you can try acting in a way that is opposite to the way you usually behave. Then, evaluate those results. If you are a people-pleaser and have a difficult time showing anger, try something new for you. Try telling someone you know when you are upset and see what happens.

If you need to be perfect to feel worthwhile, choose to do less on a task and notice the consequences. For example, if you're taking a class and have to write an essay, try this experiment — choose to write a "B" or a "C" paper this time. Don't even try to write the "A+" paper that you would prefer to.

Each time you observe yourself falling into one of these basic assumption traps, trying to be perfect, trying to be in total control, or always pleasing people, you have an opportunity to reevaluate your beliefs and change your behavior. With time and practice, you can replace these beliefs with other, more realistic and less stressful ones.

LEARNING TO FACE SITUATIONS I FEAR

Exposure Techniques for Overcoming Avoidance

The role of avoidance in your problem is complex. It is responsible for the development of your fear of certain places, because the longer you avoid a place, the harder it becomes to go there again. But, in addition to avoiding specific places, you are also avoiding the frightening sensations of panic when you are anxious. By trying to distract yourself, or to fight the sensation of panic by tensing your body or trying to force control of your feelings at all costs, your fear of having these feelings intensifies.

Your feelings of relief when you escape from those dreaded situations act to reinforce your fear of that place, and so you become more and more fixed in your determination to avoid wherever you feel anxious. The most successful way to reverse this process is exposure, that is, to go to those avoided places regardless of how you will feel when you get there.

If you put yourself in a situation you have avoided so that you can experience and learn to tolerate

the physical sensations of anxiety, you can learn to lower your fear.

This process is called *habituation.* Studies show that whatever kind of exposure you practice — prolonged (for hours at a time), gradual (a series of gradually increasing exposures), alone or with other people — the technique does work. The key to success is to approach and face what you are afraid of.

Interestingly, you may discover that what you fear most is always with you — the internal sensations your body produces when you perceive danger. But remember what we said earlier about the connection between panic and place. Approaching what you are afraid of means approaching your feelings of anxiety. It is very important to remember this when you practice exposure. *You must prepare yourself for some anxiety and be ready to cope with it in that situation.* Remind yourself that these are opportunities to practice coping strategies and will eventually help you overcome your problem once and for all.

Making an Ordered List of Situations You Avoid

Before you begin to practice exposure, make a list of situations you avoid. If there are many places you avoid, it is helpful to rank them in the order of the intensity you feel about them. Start practicing in situations where you will have the most chance of success, and later move to more difficult situations. **Regular practice is essential.** Your first attempts can be regarded as experiments to explore your present limits, so try not to be too hard on yourself or discouraged if this exercise is very difficult at first. Use the "Practice Journal" worksheet on page 37 to chart your progress.

At first, try to identify what tends to raise your anxiety level. Then see which coping strategies are most helpful for you. **Remember: the goal is to face and tolerate some anxiety without escaping from the situation.** Even if you leave, it will help you if you experience the anxiety and decrease its level to some degree. Although you can escape a feared situation at any time, if you leave while your anxiety level is high, it's best to return and reenter the situation as soon as you can to get more practice.

If you have trouble getting back into a situation in which you've panicked on a previous occasion, you may want to do some "imaginary exposure" first. Imagine yourself back in the situation and review those parts that make you most nervous, for instance, all the associated physical sensations and thoughts. Practice your rational responses and slow, gentle breathing as you imagine the situation. Continue to imagine coping until these strategies lower your anxiety to manageable levels. You might want to tape record these exercises. If so, after you describe each panic situation, leave room on the tape to imagine using your coping skills.

Another useful strategy for reentering avoided situations is to break the task of going back into small steps. For example, if you've had a bad time in elevators, you might just want to look at the elevator on the first try, and the next time press the buttons to call the elevator, and later actually get on the elevator. For others, getting on the elevator right away seems to work best. Going with a partner you trust or a therapist may also help you.

Another strategy involves exposure only to internal fear cues — the rapid heartbeat, shortness of breath, etc. Even if you're in a safe place, imagining a feared internal symptom can lead to a panic attack. It's very possible that you don't realize that what you actually have is a strong, illogical aversion to your own bodily sensations. If you can learn to bring the scary symptom to a therapist or a trusted companion in a safe situation, you can practice turning the symptom on and off using coping strategies. When the scary symptoms are under your voluntary control, a change in your heartbeat or your breathing, for example, will no longer lead to a panic attack.

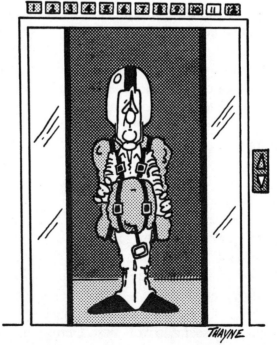

Maybe it's time to practice your exposure techniques!

SUCCESS BREEDS SUCCESS

Once you begin to have some success, it will be easier to continue on to more difficult situations, *but how you define success will be very important.* If you assume that every practice session has to be perfect, or that there is no way you could cope in a certain situation, or that trying one time is enough, your standards are too high. That means it will be very difficult to feel good about what you are doing. In the beginning, "success" might be maintaining a 7 or an 8 on your anxiety scale rather than a 10.

Give yourself credit for what you are doing! Keeping yourself at an anxiety level of 7 or 8, or watching that level rise and fall without escaping, is real progress.

Doing these exercises gives you real proof that anxiety, while uncomfortable, will not make your worst fears come true.

If you have panic attacks in crowded shopping malls or movie theaters, enter these places when they are not as crowded and gradually build up to the most crowded times. This is also evidence of progress. Another sign of progress is learning to notice reductions in your anxiety while you are in a tense situation. This will probably happen by practicing slow, even breathing and de-catastrophizing your thoughts, i.e., realizing that the worst of your fears just isn't going to happen.

Every time you experience success, write it down on a small piece of paper and put it into an empty glass jar. Watch the jar fill up with your accomplishments. When you feel discouraged, empty the jar and read about each victory. Just looking at the jar can remind you of your progress.

Record-keeping

If you will keep a record of panic situations you have been in, and the level of your anxiety from 0 to 10, as well as the state of your thinking, you will have important information about what seems to help you. If you start to monitor your anxiety before, during, and after a panic attack on the "Practice Journal" worksheet, you'll notice that *the level of your anxiety before you enter the situation in no way predicts the degree of anxiety you'll feel in that situation.* Also, it doesn't predict how well you'll cope with your feelings. But, when you are prepared to practice, you'll be ready to help yourself with the new techniques you've learned. Then, if you keep a record, it will be visual proof of your improvement. If you have a bad day, or a setback, reviewing your records can help you maintain perspective, and remind you that you have up's and down's, just like everyone else.

When you are about to enter a stressful situation or experience a frightening physical sensation, keep these new ideas in mind. We have summarized many of them on the following "Exposure Strategy List." This list has also been repeated at the back of the book. Clip out this list and carry it with you for quick reference when you're feeling anxious and uncomfortable.

PRACTICE JOURNAL

Date/Situation	Anxiety Level (0-10)	Negative Thoughts	Coping Responses	1. Rate anxiety (0-10) 2. Comments on my coping *Note and praise successes

EXPOSURE STRATEGY LIST

1. Anxiety sensations are normal physical reactions and are not harmful.
2. Focus on the rational explanations you've learned. Do not add to your sensations by dwelling on frightening thoughts.
3. Practice your slow, gentle breathing.
4. Some anxiety is normal, so when it bothers you, use your coping techniques.
5. Focus on what is really happening to you and around you — not what you are afraid might happen.
6. Wait for your fear to decrease and notice when it begins to fade. If you leave the situation, return as soon as possible to continue practice.
7. Each practice situation is an opportunity for progress.
8. Celebrate your successes no matter how small. They will add up!

Remember that when you escape or run away from a fearful situation, the anxiety grows in your mind and it will be much harder to enter that situation again. That means that your abilities to cope with anxiety will diminish or weaken. So, if you can, rather than leave, pause. Wait. Often your anxiety will subside.

If you are planning to work on your panic, try thinking of a panic situation not as one single terrible event. Instead, try to view it as a situation that has three phases of work for you in order to cope with it:

1. Preparing for the symptoms before they occur;
2. Coping with the symptoms when they occur; and
3. Reinforcing yourself for coping, and staying with the situation.

During the preparation phase, remember that coping techniques such as slow, gentle breathing, relaxation, and rational techniques will help you look at yourself and your panic symptoms a little more realistically, in addition to preparing you for the actual situation. For many people the anticipation of a panic attack is much worse than the actual panic situation itself, and these techniques can really decrease your worry about the "what if's."

When you are in a fearful situation, you'll be testing and practicing different skills, learning how effective they are for you. Measure your decreasing anxiety levels to discover which techniques are the most useful for you, and rely on them in the future. Be sure to write them down.

If you feel discomfort in the situation, whatever it is, you have a chance to deal with it. Face the internal sen-

sations you fear. Experiencing anxiety will help you realize you can tolerate it — you won't die — and you can
continue with your life. **You know you can tolerate a lot
of anxiety, because you already have!** Even severe anxiety episodes can teach you that catastrophes don't happen
just because of the way you feel. There's a very good
chance that you've underestimated your abilities to with-
stand and cope with anxiety.

It's important to acknowledge your success. Give yourself a pat on the back for trying. Success might simply be
allowing yourself to remain in the situation, experiencing the
physical sensations of anxiety while knowing that those
signs will eventually fade away. At this point staying in the
situation will be associated with *decreasing* rather than
increasing anxiety. When you can do this, a major break-
through will have been achieved.

As you gain control over anxiety, a number of changes
will take place. You will be able to focus more easily on
those parts of the situation that are enjoyable or comforting. You'll begin to realize that the catastrophes you have
been expecting won't happen. With practice, the physical
sensations of panic will begin to decline and disappear as
well. If your fear returns at any point, you understand it
now and you can handle it. You will learn that you can begin
to function in situations even while you're feeling some
level of fear, and you can appreciate that achievement. Also,
you can perform some constructive tasks even with a certain level of fear, and you may discover that performing
these tasks can help the fear from growing out of control.

When your panic attacks occur less often and your self-
confidence increases, you are free to participate in activities
you once avoided. At this point, you can examine other areas

in your life that contributed to your distress. Were you at a crisis point when the panic attacks developed? Investigating the kinds of thoughts or situations that preceded your panic attacks may shed light on conflicts and tensions you can now eliminate.

Try to identify other areas of your life that cause stress. If you're feeling trapped or uncomfortable in a relationship, this may be the time to look at what's troubling you. If you find that you are keeping your anger to yourself in your personal relationships, assertiveness training might help you comfortably let people know how you feel.

As you progress, you may find that your success in facing, and overcoming, panic will lead to a reevaluation of your entire life. Some readjustments will certainly be necessary as you are able to take more control over your life, and some of your relationships may need to be redefined. This might cause stress for you and others, but as your confidence grows, working on the other problems in your life can be tackled in just the same way you approached your anxiety problems — by looking at the situation realistically, confronting your fears, and doing some problem-solving.

As you read these pages, you may want to overcome your panic, but feel discouraged about the possibilities of succeeding. These thoughts are common and nothing to be concerned about. We encourage you to begin your program for recovery right away! Many, many others have succeeded — now it's your turn.

"Just remember... I'm not having a heart attack. My heart has to speed up to meet my body's needs during exercise. I'm just experiencing normal physical sensations. I'm okay."

My Anxiety Rating Scale

Many people with panic attacks can't discriminate different levels of anxiety. They are either calm or panicky. To help you become aware of your own intermediate levels of anxiety, fill out this form, being as specific as you can. Experiment with the coping strategies we have mentioned to discover what ones work best for you at different levels of anxiety.

When I am at Level 10 (very panicky):

    My thoughts are...

    My bodily sensations are...

    My avoidance behavior makes me...

When I am at Level 8 (on the verge of panic):

    My thoughts are...

    My bodily sensations are...

    My avoidance behavior makes me...

When I am at Level 6 (severe anxiety):

    My thoughts are...

    My bodily sensations are...

    My avoidance behavior makes me...

When I am at Level 4 (moderate anxiety):

    My thoughts are...

    My bodily sensations are...

    My avoidance behavior makes me...

When I am at Level 2 (mid anxiety):

    My thoughts are...

    My bodily sensations are...

    My avoidance behavior makes me...

My Targets for Change Checklist

1. Physical
   List the internal physical sensations you feel during panic attacks, i.e. heart palpitations, dizziness, shortness of breath.
List the three that frighten you most.

_____

_____

_____

_____

2. Cognitive
   List the thoughts you have when anticipating or experiencing a panic attack, i.e. "I'm having a heart attack," or "I'm going crazy," or "I'm losing control," etc.

_____

_____

_____

_____

3. Avoidance Behavior
   List the places or situations you avoid as a result of panicky feelings. Then list the places you enter with discomfort because of panic symptoms. Rate the degree of panic you feel on a scale of 0 to 10.

_____

_____

_____

_____

Places I avoid:

_____

_____

_____

_____

Places I enter with discomfort:

_____

_____

_____

_____

Places where I experience excitement or arousal as frightening (exercise, etc.):

_____

_____

_____

_____

Tension/Relaxation Rating Sheet
Rate from 0 (most relaxed) to 10 (most tense)

Date	Before Relaxation	After Relaxation	Events, Thoughts Physical Sensations Contributing to Stress

Notes on My Progress

2

Why Am I Having Panic Attacks Again?

How to Manage Setbacks

Many people who have learned how to handle their panic attacks believe that they are "home free." However, setbacks are a natural part of the process of overcoming anxiety reactions. In fact, setbacks are signs of improvement. After all, a setback can only happen if forward progress has occurred. Setbacks are normal, predictable, and understandable. Let's look at what setbacks are, how they happen, and what you can do about them.

WHAT A SETBACK FEELS LIKE

When you have a setback, you regress to old ways of acting and forget your new ways of thinking. Once again your feelings of panic seem out of control. Though you have experienced progress, it seems as if you're back to square one. The old pattern reasserts itself: you become anxious about your anxiety or fearful about your fear. We call this the Relapse Cycle. When that happens, you need to stop and assess your reactions. Failure to evaluate your feelings and behaviors only makes recovery more difficult.

RELAPSE CYCLE

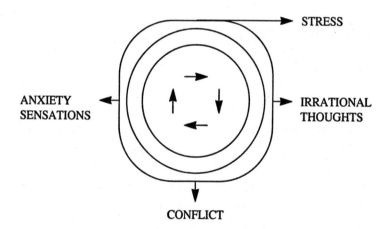

WHY DO I HAVE SETBACKS?

Often, panic sufferers set very high standards for themselves, probably higher than anyone can possibly achieve. If you're preoccupied with trying to do everything perfectly as you possibly can, with an all-or-nothing way of thinking, a small setback can easily escalate into a major catastrophe. Everyone experiences setbacks at one time or another. You will know you're on the road to recovery when you have learned to experience normal anxiety without panicking and without considering it a setback.

Inability to control anxiety perpetuates the cycle of setbacks. The "should's" and the "have-to's" press in on you. You may think, "Suppose I scream and make a fool of myself right here in front of everybody?" "Suppose I faint or have a heart attack?" "Suppose I run away?" Automatically your response is to focus on the worst possible outcome. However, you can learn ways to recognize those responses and turn them into positive experiences.

If you feel tension in relationships with your family and friends, this can cause setbacks. When you first begin to feel better, you may discover that you behave in new ways towards others, becoming more independent and self-confident. This newly found independence may surprise you and those around you — and it may cause a new and different kind of conflict. You will need to learn ways to be more assertive and direct with people about your needs and feelings instead of expressing these through symptoms of fear. Sometimes a third party can help you gain a new perspective in changing relationships. Don't be afraid to consult a trusted friend, clergyman, or professional counselor.

BREAKING FREE FROM
THE SETBACK CYCLE

The Relapse Cycle is a closed circle — it goes around and around, gaining momentum as you feel worse and worse. You can break free of this painful repetition by remembering that you have choices. This will help you move from feeling helpless to feeling empowered.

Tell yourself that this relapse is a learning opportunity. Ask yourself, "What can I learn from this experience? What can I learn about myself and my life that can push me forward in my recovery and make me stronger in the future?" Re-read your First Alert Card. It is time now for you to break free and enter the Recovery Cycle.

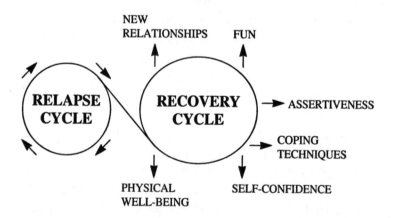

The Recovery Cycle has many options, choices, and paths of personal growth. Why not transform your fear and discomfort into a setback opportunity?

The Setback Opportunity

Instead of emphasizing everything that goes wrong and ignoring what goes right, you'll make much faster progress if you think in terms of small successes. If you've ever watched someone learn how to ski, you know that it's a process of small successes. No one expects to ski perfectly the first time. In fact, falling down is an important part of learning how to balance on skis. The learning to deal with anxiety reactions is a similar process. Each "failure" teaches you what to do differently next time. If you expect that some fear will recur, you can label the experience as an opportunity to gain information to use in the future.

Here are some common myths about setbacks. Compare them to the facts.

MYTHS ABOUT SETBACKS	FACTS ABOUT SETBACKS
1. Setbacks are my fault.	1. Setbacks are not my fault. They mean I have experienced an automatic response to stress.

MYTHS ABOUT SETBACKS	FACTS ABOUT SETBACKS
2. Setbacks mean I have to start all over.	2. I have already learned many techniques. It will take less time to re-learn the necessary tasks than the first time.
3. Setbacks mean I'm never going to get better.	3. Setbacks are signs of improvement. A setback can only come after an advance. That means I have made progress.
4. Setbacks mean the worst panic attack will come back and never leave.	4. Setbacks are only temporary occurrences.
5. There is nothing good about a setback.	5. Setbacks are opportunities to learn to manage anxiety in new ways.
6. Setbacks mean that I'm abnormal, that I'm hopeless.	6. Setbacks are proof that I'm normal, and that my progress to recovery is real. No real person can master new skills without making errors and having ups and downs.

What to Do

Imagine yourself in a situation that makes you anxious. You're beginning to worry that your anxiety will escalate into a panic attack. What can you do? Here are several very important suggestions:

1. *Challenge your thoughts.* Don't decide that a single setback means failure, or proof that you can't succeed. This kind of thinking leads to guilt and loss of self-confidence. Review your previous progress so you can feel better about yourself. Remember that occasional failures are part of the growth process.

2. *Prepare for setbacks.* Expect them to occur. Accept that some circumstances will cause you anxiety. Do not avoid your feelings, but use the situation to practice coping techniques.

3. *Practice for success.* Choose your response to a setback; you can do that now. Don't become preoccupied with negative fantasizing; think about what is really happening. You can even plan ahead, thinking about what you will do about a setback before it happens. Above all, use a setback as an opportunity to learn about yourself and how you cope with stressful situations. A positive approach increases self-confidence, makes setbacks easier to manage, and reduces the chance of future setbacks.

4. *Talk to yourself.* Pretend that you are talking to your best friend. Admit that you're having a rough time. Remind yourself that you've made progress, and that the setback problem is temporary. Talk to yourself in a soothing, comforting voice: "Could I be overreacting? What's really happening? What kinds of catastrophic thoughts am I having about the situation?"

The more you can identify your feelings, the more control you will have over them!

5. *Sort out what you are really feeling.* Other feelings, such as anger, sadness, or loneliness, can be mistaken for anxiety. Perhaps something you're not even aware of is bothering you. Since many people have setbacks during stressful periods, try to identify those times when you are vulnerable to increased anxiety. And don't forget to consider physical factors, such as lack of sleep. Above all, don't blame yourself for whatever you are feeling; focus on the external circumstances that may be causing you to feel this way.

6. *Try to do some problem-solving.* Begin by rating your anxiety. Identify what happened just before your anxiety scale began to rise. Perhaps you're only slightly uncomfortable, but you're worried that the level you're feeling right now, maybe a 3, for example, might escalate into an 8. Stop, take a step back, and think. Your problem-solving efforts will teach you to recognize what causes your own setbacks. Then, you can develop a plan of action to deal with these new discoveries. And you can remind yourself that "competence breeds confidence."

7. *Review the records of your progress.* Your records are the visible proof of your progress. When you have a setback, look at those records; they'll remind you that you made it through these difficult times before, and so you can do it again.

8. *Stick with it.* Face the setback head on — give yourself the courage to overcome the associated anxiety. Review your records. Congratulate yourself on the progress you've made. Keep negative feelings in perspective.

9. *Stay active.* Don't allow a setback to disrupt your progress for long. Pace yourself. No one can tell you how quickly your problems will be solved. Return to the anxiety-producing situation as soon as possible. Practice the coping strategies that have worked in the past.

10. *Get support from friends, family, and /or a therapist.* Share your feelings of frustration and disappointment.

11. *Remember that these attacks can be overcome.* Many, many others have succeeded and so can you!

A New Attitude about Setbacks

Setbacks are natural; they are to be expected. After all, there is no such thing as a perfectly problem-free recovery. You've already begun the process of recovery and have many reasons to be proud of yourself. You are learning to view yourself as one who can cope. Now you can learn to replace your negative definition of a setback with positive understanding. As you progress, setbacks will occur less often, and you will begin to recognize them as minor disturbances, part of the normal ups and downs of living. And when you accept some anxiety in life as manageable, you'll handle these occasions more easily than ever.

3

How Family and Friends Can Help

Do's and Don't's for Those Who Care

Your family and friends may sometimes contribute to your stress. They may often have to deal with the consequences of your fear, just as you do, and they can lapse into feelings of frustration, helplessness, resentment, irritation, and even anger.

Often, however, all that family and friends really want to know is, "What can I do to help?" Therefore, we recommend the following list of helpful suggestions, as a result of listening and learning from our clients. So, here's a list of do's and don't's for those who are closest to you.

1. DON'T criticize. Sufferers of panic attacks have real physical symptoms. They are probably more critical of themselves than you are. Remember that negative

comments can contribute to slowing down their progress by adding stress and making them feel guilty for their feelings!

2. DO encourage rather than shame or embarrass them. They are already tackling a difficult situation, so positive support will pay off for everyone in the end.

3. DON'T induce guilt when the anxious person is unable to do certain things. It is hard for them to deal with their limitations anyway, and adding guilt will only alienate you from the person you most want to help.

4. DON'T express disappointment, anger, or frustration if a setback occurs. When trying to overcome a problem like this, every effort is an accomplishment, with the potential for other, greater accomplishments in the future.

5. DO notice and compliment their efforts to conquer their fear, as well as their actual successes. Your affirmation will help build their confidence.

6. DO be empathic. Try to understand the problem from their point of view. They don't need your pity, but your help, your encouragement, and your support.

7. DO be willing to accompany them on practice sessions if they ask you to. This means going along because you want to help, not because you feel obligated.

8. DO be quick to point out their positive qualities. Give them the same consideration you would want for yourself.

9. DO listen when they need to talk. It can be a great relief for them to share their distress. Also, listening becomes an opportunity to gently encourage their attempts to cope.

10. DO allow them to be in charge whenever you can. The ability to make decisions and take action is a real aid to self-confidence and helps them realize that control is possible.

11. DO avoid surprises. Let them know what is going to happen and when, so they can make plans to deal with any panic that may arise.

12. DO help them identify their successes. Change can be so gradual that improvements may go unnoticed and a sense of progress is very important.

13. DO work with them to identify family patterns, situations, or concerns that may contribute to the problem. Try to notice and improve any interactions between you that are detrimental to their growth and independence.

14. DO be consistent. Recognize that there will probably be changes as they are better able to handle anxiety and stress. Try not to be threatened by the prospect

of their increased self-confidence or potential changes in your relationship. Seek family therapy or marital counseling if necessary.

15. DO be patient! Maybe more than anything, it will help if your loved ones know that, when they finally overcome these attacks, you will be there for them.

(Adapted with permission from an article in the *Greater Boston Phobia Society Newsletter.*)

4

It Feels So Good to Feel Good Again!

Personal Stories of Recovery

MARGARET'S STORY

I awoke one night out of a sound sleep with a racing, irregular heartbeat, difficulty breathing, and an incredible feeling of terror. I was twenty-seven then, and it was my first panic attack. I was petrified. My husband was out of town on a business trip, and I thought I was dying! When the attack finally passed, I went back to sleep and didn't think too much about it because it didn't happen again.

About a year later I began having headaches and dizzy spells every day. I spent a week in the hospital having tests and all the doctors and tests said I was "fine." However, little by little, more symptoms of panic attacks began to occur.

My husband and I loved to go out to dinner and it was about the only time we got to see each other, but then I began having problems in restaurants. I'd get a severe headache, feel faint and short of breath, and I even got nauseated. Basically, I started getting terrified. As a result, we stopped going to restaurants. Next, it progressed to me staying away from church, shopping, and friends' homes. The most frightening thing to me was that I was beginning to have panic attacks at home. Nowhere was safe.

Meanwhile, my children were getting older and more involved with sports and other after-school activities. My husband would have to take time off from work to drive them or I would have to depend on my very friendly neighbors. I really hated this dependency on other people and the fact that all these people had such control over my life. My husband had to take the kids to dentists, doctors, haircuts, etc. Our entire Saturdays were spent doing errands I could have done during the week if I could have driven. And I was always being told by my family and friends that I *should* be driving . . . and why wasn't I?

I really wanted to drive, but I was afraid to even be a passenger in a car. I was really caught in a dilemma. I wanted the freedom and control of being able to drive, but I was afraid that if I did learn to drive, I'd never see my husband. It seemed that our Saturday errands were the only times we had to ourselves, together.

I went to my internist and he suggested that I see a psychotherapist. I saw both for two years and was on medication, but progress was slow. Finally, in desperation I turned to another medical doctor and psychotherapist. The thing that really irritated me was that I was having difficulty handling stress at this time in my life, when for so many years before, I had lots of serious responsibilities and I handled them well. Now my life was falling apart.

With the new doctor I went through all the physical exams again to rule out any heart or neurological problems. Everything was okay physically and it was suggested that I join an agoraphobic therapy group. That was the first time the word *agoraphobia* was used to describe my problem. I was a little skeptical about group therapy because I'm very shy and not a joiner. But, to my surprise I found that I was actually participating in the group and feeling good about it. The first and most important thing I learned was that I couldn't die from a panic attack. So, every day the fear of dying was greatly lessened. With that out of the way, I was able to concentrate on how I was going to handle and maybe beat this problem.

One big step on this road to recovery was getting my driver's license. Instead of thinking about how scared I was, I took it a step at a time, got my learner's permit, tried to practice every day, took some lessons, and got my license in September on the first day of school, just in time to pick up my daughter. The look on her face when she saw me there to pick her up was my reward for all the anxiety attacks I had while learning to drive.

I've had my license for just a short time now and I can't believe the difference in my life already. The sense of freedom and control is almost euphoric. To be able to drive myself around is the greatest feeling. I finally feel like a grown-up again. Not only that, my husband is spending more time with us as a family, and we are making more time for the two of us.

(Excerpted with permission from the *Greater Boston Phobia Society Newsletter.*)

BETSY'S STORY

My panic attacks started two and a half years ago. I was
going to college and I began to have what I thought were
colds. Later, it turned out that they were actually panic
attacks. I would break out in a sweat for some unknown
reason, and my heart would race. Also, I didn't realize I
was hyperventilating, but I was. That made it worse, so I
would call up my husband at work and he'd say, "Now
breathe, sit down, calm down." But, as soon as I hung up,
I would hyperventilate again. It just sort of mushroomed
into what I thought was a real physical disorder.

Nothing really helped. I just got worse. I got to a
point where, when I would try to drive and a plane flew
over, I would get scared. I would just grab the wheel and
shake. Eventually, I didn't leave my house. I avoided
anything that took me out into the world by myself — anything I had to do alone, anything that required any sort of
driving. I didn't want to leave my little cocoon, because
that's where I felt safe — but that didn't even last long. I
began to have problems with digestion. Then my appetite
just disappeared. I couldn't seem to process food. Also,
I had a lot of numbness in my arm which worried me a
great deal, and many times I felt dizzy. I decided the problem must be physical, so I began to go to doctors, but all
the medical examinations came back normal.

When I started reading books on panic attacks and
learned more about the symptoms I was having, I began
to get a little better and my husband became more willing
to go along with whatever I needed.

I began to see a counselor, and that was when I learned
I had a need for approval. I had to be a good girl! In the

process of going to therapy and trying to follow the practical advice I got, I challenged myself enough so that I began to see a little progress. Even though I thought I would never get better, I still kept trying to take it a step further each time. I wanted to come back to my therapy session and tell my counselor that I had done better. Eventually, I just did it for myself.

As I began to make progress, there was one thing I was still afraid of. I thought I couldn't cope with working and having someone be dependent on me. Luckily, I just got thrown into work. My husband's office needed a receptionist. I had the ability to do what they needed, and we needed the money, so I said yes without thinking. When I started working, I realized there was nothing to panic over and so within a week, I had the routine down and was doing fine. I also made some wonderful friends and was doing a good job.

Now, as I drive to work, I think of the days when I drove the freeway just gripping the wheel in a state of panic for fear I would pass out. I would see spots in front of my eyes. (My counselor told me this was from my forced breathing.) Every once in a while, I still discover myself holding on to the wheel with a vise grip, so I try to pry my fingers loose. I quickly remind myself that I'm okay, and I begin to relax. Now the freeway is like an old friend. It is my road home.

My advice to anyone having symptoms like the ones I used to have is to keep trying and never give up, because it's only by trying again and again that you get through this kind of ordeal. Just one step further each time, and eventually you'll make the trip!

RANDY'S STORY

I have fears of going in elevators, flying, and tunnels. The tremendous fear of going through tunnels was because I was afraid the tunnels would collapse. About twelve years ago, I had to go to a seminar in New York, and my room was on the thirty-third floor. Being that high bothered me, and also taking the elevators to get up there. They were very small elevators and very confining. The room itself seemed like a box. The windows couldn't even open. I spent most of the night down in the lobby talking to the hotel staff. Then, I got very nervous and wanted to leave and come home. I couldn't fly home, so I took the train. I hadn't flown anywhere in twenty years.

Finally, I decided I had to do something about my fears. My daughter moved to Washington. Even though my wife wanted to fly because she never had, we drove and we avoided the Baltimore Tunnel by going over a bridge. This trip was the last straw that spurred me to get help so I could get over these difficulties. I went to a therapist, and together we started going to an elevator nearby that went up five floors. First, I entered with the therapist, and then I began to go by myself.

I discovered that the first thing I did when I went into an elevator was to look at the indicator showing which floor we were on. I wanted to know how fast I could get out — I was looking for an escape. Instead, I was encouraged to focus on feeling comfortable in the elevator and realizing I was safe there. So, that's what I did. Now, when I go into an elevator, I don't worry about it stalling or breaking down. If I do get a momentary twinge, I can settle down, because I know that nothing terrible will happen.

Next, my wife and I began to go through tunnels. We started at times when the tunnel would be less crowded and worked up to peak traffic times. Taking slow breaths from my belly, rather than from my chest, helped a great deal. I began to breath as if I were blowing through a straw — slowly and gently. The breathing was a big factor. Now there are many other relaxation things that I just do automatically.

The first few times the tunnels were frightening! But as I went through, I overcame that fright just by confronting it. The belly breathing and listening to a comforting tape were helpful while I was going through, and before I knew it, I had made it through. One time, coming back from Washington, we took a different route and headed into a tunnel I didn't know was there. I didn't tell my wife, but my anxiety level was about a 5 or 6 right before we entered the tunnel. However, there was no alternative but to go through it, so I used the breathing method and settled down. I knew I was panicking because the tunnel was unfamiliar and I wasn't ready for it. Anyway, I went through it and I was okay, so I realized I didn't need to be frightened of tunnels anymore.

I had done so well with elevators and tunnels that the therapist and I decided to take a shuttle flight from Boston to New York. I was afraid, but I was also determined to do it! On the way to the airport I was very nervous, but when I saw the plane, I imagined myself being inside and unafraid. It also helped to visualize the pilot and the big windows in the cockpit. I had a tranquilizer in my pocket, but I didn't use it. I didn't even order a drink. However, talking with the therapist helped, as we approached the terminal and while we were on the plane.

What bothered me the most about being in the plane was the fact that they were going to close the doors. I knew I would feel extra confined when the doors closed. My therapist said, "You really wouldn't want the doors to be open when you were flying, would you?" That really got to me. That would be no way to fly! So, I immediately settled down, and started doing my gentle breathing. Not only did I actually enjoy the flight, I felt accomplishment.

Later, I discovered that flying is very exciting to me. I actually love the take-off and like to land, too! I realized that my deep fear was that I would panic and run up and down the aisles like a crazy person totally out of control, but finally I became convinced that I wouldn't really do that. I've flown many times since then. We have flown to see my daughter a number of times now. I fly whenever I can, my wife flies with me, and we both love it! My advice to other people is not to worry too much about panicking. If a panicky thought comes to your mind, immediately be sure you're breathing properly, and change to a positive, more realistic thought. The most important thing I can say is, whatever you're afraid about, if you want to do it, *just do it !*

RONELLE'S STORY

In the seventh grade was when I first started having panic attacks. Looking back, I can see that I had a lot of separation anxiety. I never wanted to stay overnight at a friend's house. I was very conscious of my body as I got a little older, and always worried about getting sick.

When the first attack occurred, I stayed out of school for a while. That was the time I think I was the most agoraphobic, as far as having trouble even getting out of the house at all. I was really afraid that something disastrous would happen to me physically, like I would die or have a heart attack, or something else horrendous. So, as I started having more and more panic attacks, the idea that I was going crazy or would make a fool of myself in front of the whole class made me feel totally out of control. I started seeing a therapist, and between my mom and him, I eventually went back to school, but my problem sort of cycled up and down throughout my school years.

Going to college was really a big deal to me — could I do it? I really associated school with panic attacks, so I always thought that once I was out of school, I would be free, that the problem would go away. I wouldn't have the pressure to go somewhere everyday. College was the first time I had ever left home, and it was a time when things got much worse. I went home quite often because, at that point, home was still a pretty safe place.

However, when I got out of college, the panic attacks didn't go away. When I started to think, "What am I going to do with my life?" my stress increased. I didn't have a clue about what I wanted to do. About a year after I graduated, when I started getting serious about my future, I started having trouble again. Things got as bad as I can ever remember. I began to worry about going crazy and never being able to function in life.

My heart rate was the main thing with me — issues around breathing and not having enough air. I wasn't hyperventilating in the sense of having to breathe in a paper bag, but I've been told that I definitely hyperventilate without being aware of it. I would breathe way too fast and get a lot of weird body aches. I became depressed, convinced that nothing was going to change, and I would never be normal. Finally, I got to the point where I thought, "I've got to find somebody who knows about panic!" I was very depressed and just couldn't deal with the attacks anymore. I felt nervous everywhere — I didn't even feel safe at home now.

My mother, whom I felt really close to, got some information for me, and I began to research it some more. The turning point came when I finally found some specialists in panic disorder who could help me.

Learning how to breathe was the biggest and most important factor for me. It was really powerful for me to know that my breathing was causing a lot of the symptoms. It was really cool to be able to focus on my breathing and get control. The idea that, "Okay, I'm in control and if the symptoms get worse, I can do something to feel better" was very important to me.

I had a lot of problems quieting my mind for the more complex relaxation skills, so I learned to sort of cue myself to relax. Practicing has helped even though I was convinced it wouldn't. I've been getting better gradually, and I've become a little more objective about the situation by reminding myself that my body is not doing the same thing my mind is thinking. Also, I look at what is really going on. "Is there really any danger? No, there isn't some horrific thing. Things are okay." It's been fascinating for me to learn that my body is doing the right thing, but the messages I'm sending it are wrong. Now I have a habit of just saying, "It's okay. I feel stressed and tense, but I don't need to panic."

I think at this point I've internalized a lot of what I've learned in counseling. Now I can come up with many of the same thoughts on my own. In the past, I used to lose all that learning and feel that I was going to fall apart and have the worst panic attack I'd ever had. Then, something new happened to me. I began to deal with these scary thoughts as they came up, trying to talk back to these thoughts. I constantly reminded myself that I really don't have any proof of disaster. When anxiety starts to come up, I tell myself that it's an old habit and that I know it's going to be okay.

In my opinion, the most important step in recovery is to get help from people who really know about the problem, and then really educate yourself about it. Knowing what is happening to you makes it less terrifying. Also, worrying about what might happen was always the worst part. I was afraid of the scary ideas in my own head that I had no basis for. Now I know that I was afraid of things I didn't need to be afraid of.

JIM'S STORY

My first panic attack hit me in 1979 and it was a living hell. It came out of nowhere and hit me at work one day. I got up right away and went outside the building for some fresh air. I felt better, so I went back in, but the next day I had two or three attacks at work. The third day I didn't want to go back. Then the attacks began to spread to gas stations, shopping malls, stores, and restaurants. I'd get nauseated, very disoriented, and dizzy. My eyes would get blurry and I couldn't even see my way to the door, so I'd sort of feel my way out. I'd start sweating and get cold and clammy, trying to get out of the store and, believe me, I would never go back. I thought I was losing my mind!

I gave up using credit cards when I wanted to buy something, because they took too long to process. I used to go to happy hour with my girlfriend, but now I went only if she drew me a floor plan of the place with all the exits and where we were going to sit. If that table wasn't free, we didn't go in!

A doctor gave me tranquilizers, which I took for eight months. The only thing I could do was to drive to work and home. Finally, I didn't want to try anything. I slept from four in the afternoon until dinner and then went right back to bed. Sleep was my escape.

After doing some reading on the subject, I thought I was going to be able to handle panic attacks, but when I got married and moved out of state, the attacks came back and were more intense than ever. The old symptoms came back and I couldn't work. I was even having panic attacks in the house. Totally overwhelmed, I called one of the local hospitals who referred me to someone.

This counselor showed me how to grade the intensity of my panic. That was helpful, because I always assumed that it was at its highest level. In reality, some attacks were less severe than others.

One night, I went to a pub with some friends and I was very anxious, but I did relaxation exercises and deep breathing, trying to calm myself. When I joined in the conversation around the table, the anxiety would rise again, but I did the relaxation again too. It wasn't comfortable at all. I either wanted to have a panic attack or wanted it to stop. At that point, I called my therapist and she pointed out that for the first time I was able to control the anxiety. Also, for the first time, I saw that making progress didn't mean I had to be 100 percent better. After that, everything started to get better. Now I could control the panic enough to give me the confidence to practice. Finally, I could go wherever I wanted to, a restaurant, the store, or the bank, and I could even stay there when it was most crowded.

Once, after a few months of counseling and then getting a job, I went to a restaurant to have lunch. I ended up staying four hours, because I was so happy to be in a restaurant and really enjoying it. It was such a high!

The panicky thoughts were the last thing to go. After the panic was gone, the thoughts were still there. Now, I talk to myself and say, "You've been fine for a long time. If an attack comes again, you know what to do." I know I will never, never be as bad as I was before. That's because I know too much about it now. I know the necessary steps to calm myself. To anyone who is suffering panic attacks, what I want to tell them is, "You can get better...and you are not alone."

PAM'S STORY

The thought that I was a perfectionist never really occurred to me, because nothing I did was perfect! In fact, the flaws, mistakes, goofs, or whatever, were always glaringly apparent, at least to me. Every time something wasn't right, I thought, "THEY will see and THEY will know." I don't know who "they" were, and I don't know why I cared so much about what others thought. I do know that my dad told me that I could do anything if I wanted to do it bad enough, so somehow I guess I thought imperfections meant I hadn't tried hard enough.

I had reached a point in my life where I was doing a lot of things and always trying to do more. Mentally, I felt like I could do anything, but my body started sending me signals that said, "Hey, wait a minute. Not so fast." But, since I believed that my mind should control my body, I really didn't even listen. And when I started getting weird physical sensations, like feeling that my head was in a vise, or getting dizzy and seeing spots in front of my eyes, I thought I must have some kind of exotic illness.

Finally, on an out-of-town business trip, I went completely out of control. I was afraid of absolutely everything. I couldn't eat or sleep, and when I got up to give a speech, as I'd done so many times before, I just froze. My whole body went rigid. After that, the only thing I could think of to do was to force myself to try to stay in control of everything and always be on guard, prepared for the worst. After all, I thought, if I can't perform at 100 percent in my job, I will get kicked out and never asked back.

Back home, my family doctor examined me and then suggested I see a therapist. I was absolutely shocked! It took most of the summer for me to get up the courage to go see one, but my symptoms just kept getting worse and worse. Then I talked to a couple of friends who shared some really important things with me. One told me about her experience with fear after almost dying from pneumonia, and her symptoms sounded a lot like what I was going through. The other friend told me about her struggle with panic attacks, which frankly I had hardly even heard of before. Then she said, "If you really want to get well, leave no stone unturned." I'll never forget those words. I went home and dialed the therapist for an appointment.

Sometimes what I learned from the therapist still amazes me. How could I have missed the fact that I had this huge amount of "shoulds"? I *should* look good, I *should* always do my best at every moment, I *should* always be on time and never make a mistake and be energetic, happy, and above all, I *should* be able to do it all at once, all the time. I took these "shoulds" very seriously, so if my husband and I were going to have a dinner party, I would go into an incredibly high gear, making sure the food would be perfect, the house spotless, even the kids' rooms upstairs! Then, there was such enormous tension in my body during these events that the physical fatigue was unbelievable! But, as I said, it still amazes me that I had to learn that I didn't have to do all this and I had to learn it from an objective outsider, a therapist.

I began practicing physical relaxation, especially walking outside, slowly and freely — kind of like ambling. Then I started practicing *not* doing certain things. Once I even had company over without vacuuming! Not one person seemed to notice, so I pointed out my "dirty" carpet and they still couldn't see anything wrong. I discovered that I was the one who was putting the pressure on myself. No one else made the "to do" list but me.

I continued therapy for about six months and some really encouraging things happened along the way. My behavior was changing in positive ways and was being noticed by other people. My husband commented about how much more human I seemed to be and that freed him up to be much more open and free with me. People I had known for many years said it appeared that I was going through some sort of spiritual transformation — a beautiful awakening of my soul.

I don't have real panic attacks anymore, although I still have anxiety now and then, but I accept that as okay. After all, I keep reminding myself, I'm only human — I'm not perfect. The real key, for me at least, is learning that you are creating the anxiety and panic attacks yourself and, in the end, only you can get yourself out. Attacks aren't something to be ashamed of; they are something to be worked through and overcome.

You know, I wouldn't have chosen to go through all the pain and suffering I have. However, I'm not sure I would be feeling as satisfied and good about myself as I do now if I hadn't had this experience and then learned to work through it. Can you believe it? I'm now one of the people on the other side!

JANE'S STORY

A strange thing happened to me on a short, one-hour plane trip. As the plane rumbled down the taxiway, my neck stiffened up, my heart started to race, and my mouth felt like cotton. Then my head felt heavy, but I also felt dizzy. The pilot announced we were all clear for take-off, and powered down on the throttle. I couldn't swallow, I couldn't breathe, I couldn't think. As the 727 lifted off the runway, I couldn't even make out the words my husband was saying to me. My brain froze and my body belonged to somebody else.

Then, in less than sixty seconds, the plane was climbing steadily, and I felt a wave of relaxation sweep over me.

I took a deep breath, shuddered, and I was fine again. Later, I realized it was a textbook panic attack, but for the next sixteen years, my panic experience developed into a full-blown phobia of flying. I did fly from time to time, but I continued to have major panic attacks, so bad that for days ahead, I was nearly incoherent and nonfunctional.

Over the years, I fine-tuned my panic to a sixty-second period from the time the airplane tires lift off the ground to when the plane begins to level off to a more gradual climb. I could joke about it, but I was terrified of those sixty seconds. I tried everything to relax . . . I took Valium, I drank Scotch, I read trashy sex stories . . . I tried every diversion I could think of, but when those tires lifted off, I went into the ozone layer! My husband was wonderful, but he couldn't give me the magic words to stop the way I was feeling. What was I afraid of? After the first panic attack, I guess I was afraid that same feeling would happen and I began to anticipate it.

When it continued to happen, I developed a behavior pattern that I didn't know how to change, and it locked in.

The final straw came when I won a ten-day, all expenses paid trip to Europe and passed it up because I couldn't fly. I decided to get therapy and lick this thing once and for all. "Do you worry about other things besides flying?" was the first question the therapist asked. Ha! I could write a book on worry and anxiety. During the next few weeks, I discovered that my habit of worry was another learned behavior, and the anxiety I constantly experienced was the result of a steady flow of adrenalin, triggered by all that unnecessary worry.

I learned from my parents to worry about things I couldn't control. My father worried about going broke and ending up in the "poorhouse" and talked about this incessantly. He also worried about aging and becoming helpless. Since I was a baby boomer, the threat of nuclear war was another ever-present danger.

My parents were not warm and loving, but they rewarded me for excellence. So, I became an overachiever, afraid of disappointing my parents and teachers, and later, my employers, friends, and spouse. Achieving became my way of being recognized and validated. In therapy, I confronted issues such as, Did I willingly promote my fear of flying as a means to get sympathy and attention? Did I cling to it as a way of being a special person? Was I afraid of being healthy and just like everyone else? It became clear that before I could learn any new behaviors about flying, I had to take the difficult first step to begin to prove to myself that I was an okay person on my own merit. I had to learn to trust myself and my emotions and reactions, and that it was okay to say, "No, I don't want to do that," or "Gee, I don't know the answer."

The first time I flew successfully, I was ecstatic. I closed my eyes, took gentle, deep breaths, and gave in to the easy motion. When I opened my eyes, I was someplace else. I have the tools at my command now, but I don't want ever to slip backwards, and that takes practice with my newly learned relaxation techniques, imagining myself on a plane, eyes closed, and breathing steadily, deeply. These and other relaxing exercises have helped with everyday stresses and insomnia.

I have learned to fly again, literally as well as figuratively. And, as a bonus, I've stopped worrying about nuclear bombs and the poorhouse.

CHERYL'S STORY

I was in the movie theater when my first panic attack hit me. I started to get up at the end of the film and a terrible feeling came over me. I felt like I was going to faint or die or something. When I got home, the dizziness didn't go away for a couple days. My doctor took some tests, but they all came back negative, so he said it was probably a panic attack. A few weeks later, I started having trouble going to sleep, because I felt like I was choking. It was like I had a big lump in my throat and dizziness even when I was lying down. It was really scary.

Next, problems started with driving. I got dizzy on the way to work and on the way to the beauty shop. My throat would get tight and I'd get dizzy again. I felt okay all day while I was working, but I wanted to run out of there a lot of times and just go home. My family kept saying, "Just hang in there. If you go home, you're going to feel even worse."

Then I began to see a counselor and I found out that I had actually been avoiding escalators for twenty years! I would walk up a flight of stairs instead of taking the escalator, afraid that I might fall off. The counselor went into the stores with me and showed me breathing exercises and how to get back on the escalator. I kept talking to myself, telling myself that people don't fall off escalators, so there's really no danger of that. There's a normal fear when you hesitate to get on, but that doesn't mean you're going to fall. Eventually, I was able to go on one by myself.

I used the same breathing and talking to myself to get over my fear of driving. Now, in fact, I do most of the driving when I go with other women to square dancing and other activities. Anytime I feel my anxiety begin to rise, I start the breathing exercises and talking to myself, and I can convince myself that everything is okay.

Sometimes I still have a little trouble sleeping, but I've even been able to work around that. I just get up and read a book, instead of lying there thinking about panic.

I feel like I'm really doing great now. I used to be afraid of so many things, but now I feel that I'm living again. I think I've come a long way.

NANCY'S STORY

What got to me was a real dread of being sick and throwing up. In first grade, a classmate got sick and it really bothered me. The only incident I can recall that I can trace it to was when I was out visiting with my mother at one of her friend's, and somehow my mother communicated some disapproval or embarrassment that affected me. That's not to lay the blame on my mother — it's just that I was impressionable. In the following years, I was nervous that I might get sick and very nervous around other people, thinking they might get sick.

In elementary school, the rambunctious boys wanted to race to see who could drink their milk the fastest. Invariably, one of them would get sick as a result. I hated that, and I hated lunch hour. Also, I always wanted to sit nearest the door of the classroom, so I could escape to the restroom if I needed to. This carried on all through high school and college.

The problems only got worse as an adult when I was under stress. I went through a divorce and it really got bad. I could only eat at home. Restaurants have always been a constant source of problems for me. There was the stress of the problem and then the stress of hiding it from every body. If I got asked out, then I'd think, "How am I going to deal with it?"

Once I had a particularly bad business trip. I was with a group of people and someone got the flu. Even though I wasn't sick, I really got into a panic and the whole trip was unbearable. After I got home, I felt like I couldn't deal with it any longer. I'm talking about twenty-nine years of having this problem. I decided that it was about time I really put this problem away.

I started therapy and it helped get my scary thoughts under control. I began to say things like, "Okay, what would happen if you actually became sick?" That made me realize that it was more the embarrassment, the public humiliation than anything. The next step was to say, "Well, you could live through getting sick, so what?" It didn't seem so catastrophic when I began to see things in a new way. It wasn't as if I woke up one day and said, "Wow, I'm cured!" It took awhile to change and then awhile for all the new thoughts to really sink in.

Now if I'm feeling vulnerable, I'll say, "What's the worst thing that can happen?" It's important to know how to reassure yourself. The worst part about having panic attacks is being so embarrassed about it. Shame can really get in the way. Reading books about panic helped though, because I realized I wasn't that unusual. I found out that a lot of people have panic, and about weirder things than

I have. Things I was so mortified about that I wouldn't even talk about them are not so unusual. Now I consider myself a normal person. It was hard trying to hide this deep, dark secret. It's a relief to have all that in the past.

TERRI'S STORY

I've had anxiety situations most of my life. As a child I was afraid to sleep over at a friend's house, afraid of summer camp, afraid of leaving my parents. The first semester away at college it all hit me. After final exams, I was going home to be with my family and I had an unbelievable panic attack on the airplane.

After college, I became practically house-bound. I missed work for three months. I started avoiding more and more until I just couldn't do anything. I was too afraid to tell anyone about it, because I thought there was something wrong with me. I was anxious anywhere, everywhere, anytime.

I tried to explain what was happening to my boyfriend. I told him, "It feels like I'm on a little bridge on the top of a cliff and people are saying, 'Just walk off. Don't worry. Everything will be okay.'" I would think in my head, "How can they tell me that everything is going to be okay when I'm going to walk off this cliff and die?"

I went to a counselor, but at first, I couldn't even get to the floor where the office was because I couldn't take the elevator. I remember thinking, "Well, it can't be any worse than I'm feeling right now." Even being in the counselor's office scared me, that's how bad it was.

I began to relax very gradually. It went from one situation to another. The dizziness I feared went away with the breathing exercises I learned. Also, I had to expect not to feel confident about a situation that had been scary before. I just had to believe that I would be okay.

Worrying about things beforehand was the biggest thing. Things were never, ever as bad as I imagined them to be. I tried to figure out what the worst realistic outcome would be, and then decide what I could do about it. Then I realized that I could handle whatever might happen.

The thing people need to know is that, even though things will go up and down, meaning better and worse, you'll never go as far back as you were before you started working on the anxiety attacks. I wanted to write these things down, because otherwise they just get forgotten.

I realized that a lot of the panic had to do with being a perfectionist. I was trying to be very fast-paced, trying to do too many things at once, accommodating everyone else in my life and never saying no. When I began to read books about panic attacks, I kept thinking, "Hey, this is me! This is exactly what I'm feeling!" I had such bizarre feelings and then, when I read about them, I felt, "Hey, I'm not nuts after all. They're not going to lock me up because I tell them about this." It was a huge relief.

While you are reading this book and my story, remember, you don't have to trust completely. Just leave open the option that there's a chance you'll get out of this. You don't have to feel like there is absolutely no hope. You can believe that since other people got out, you can too.

Notes on My Progress

Appendix 1

How to Find Professional Help

If you reside in the Greater Boston or San Diego areas, the authors of this book are available for information, referral, and relaxation tapes.

In the Greater Boston area, contact:

> Carol Goldman, LICSW
> 29 Commonwealth Avenue, Suite 809
> Boston, MA 02116
> (617) 236-1232

In the San Diego area, contact:

> Shirley Babior, LCSW, MFCC
> Co-Director, Center for Anxiety and Stress
> Treatment
> 4350 Executive Drive, Suite 204
> San Diego, CA 92121
> (619) 458-1066

For other parts of the country, the Anxiety Disorders Association of America has a National Treatment Directory, which lists treatment programs throughout the nation. For more information write or call:

Anxiety Disorders Association of America
6000 Executive Blvd., Suite 200
Rockville, MD 20852
(301) 231-9350

If there are no therapists listed in the directory in your area, ask local professional societies for names of psychologists, social workers, and psychiatrists. If there is a college or university nearby, the counseling department may be willing to make referrals. You can also help educate local therapists by sharing this handbook with them.

When you locate a potential therapist, the following questions may be useful to you before you decide to begin treatment:

1. What is the therapist's basic approach to treatment? Does it involve exposure to panic-associated situations?
2. What additional kinds of treatment are offered?
3. Does the standard course of treatment have a set length? Is there any follow-up?
4. What are the phobia-related training and experiences of the therapist(s)?
5. What is the definition of success in this program?
6. How much does the treatment cost? Will my health insurance cover any of it?

Good Luck!

(Adapted from *National Treatment Directory* of the Anxiety Disorders Association of America.)

Appendix 2

How Therapists Can Use This Book

Overcoming Panic Attacks can be a useful adjunct to pharmacotherapy or psychotherapy. If you are interested in familiarizing yourself with the professional literature on which these strategies are based, a bibliography is available on written request.

As with all anxiety disorders, a thorough medical examination is required before entering exposure treatment. Physical disorders may be present. Specifically, a physician should always be consulted regarding the appropriateness and speed with which an exposure treatment can be carried out.

This manual may be helpful in the following ways:

• Assign it as bibliotherapy to panic-disordered clients.

• Ask your client to fill out the "My Targets for Change Checklist." This assessment instrument will help identify physical, cognitive, and avoidance behaviors that are targets for change. The section on avoidance behaviors will help you construct an exposure hierarchy. Each feared situation, for example, can be entered on a 3" x 5" card or a First Alert Card, arranged with the easiest task first and the most difficult last. Your client can practice exposure by working on one or two cards at a time, moving on to a more difficult task after mastering easier ones.

• Have your client fill out "My Anxiety Rating Scale" at the beginning of treatment. Then, have him or her rate and re-rate levels of anxiety (0-10) during exposure practice using this initial key, and refer to it often to check on the reliability of your client's subjective ratings. This training tool can help your client apply coping strategies at various levels of anxiety and discover when they are most effective. In addition, it can identify specific catastrophic thoughts that need to be changed.

• The "Tension/Relaxation Rating Sheet" will help your client develop relaxation skills. Ask your client to practice relaxation skills daily and to rate anxiety levels before and after practice. This relaxation feedback is an important gauge of the usefulness of these techniques for this client and helps to determine whether these exercises are being performed correctly. They may also help to heighten your client's awareness of the difference between tension and relaxation, and regular reports can help identify daily stressors. Once identified, appropriate therapeutic interventions (couples therapy, assertiveness training, career counseling, family therapy, etc.) can be explored. In addition, for those clients who experience tension while doing the exercises, you can help them restructure their thoughts about the danger of these sensations.

• The "Practice Journal" is an essential component of exposure practice. It can also be used to collect baseline data for assessment purposes if your client is instructed to fill out columns 1, 2, and 3 only (i.e., "Date/Situation," "Anxiety Level," and "Negative Thoughts," respectively). During treatment, this record-keeping directs the client's focus towards coping strategies and outcome measures. In the comments columns, help your client praise his or her own efforts and identify ways to improve these efforts in future situations. Periodic review of the practice journals will highlight the client's improvement over time.

Appendix 3

How Support Groups Can Use This Book

If you are in a support group, it is important that you focus on strategies for change. This handbook suggests various coping techniques for that purpose and explains their relevance to phobic anxiety. Your group may choose to practice relaxation together. You may record for one another the muscle relaxation exercises or the scripts. Use the "Practice Journal" to determine your success on the "My Targets for Change Checklist," and compare the places you avoid. Perhaps you can accompany one another when you practice exposure.

There are many ideas here that you might discuss as a group. Assign a certain chapter for a particular meeting; you might even invite a professional to the same meeting for additional insight.

Embarking on this program together can be easier than attempting it alone. Try to use your group as a "mutual aid society," rather than one in which you simply trade war stories. Remember that members can help one another even if they avoid entirely different situations, because the fear of internal physical sensations is the essential phobia for everyone in your group.

(Cut along dotted line.)

EXPOSURE STRATEGY LIST

1. Anxiety sensations are normal physical reactions and are not harmful.
2. Do not add to these sensations by having frightening thoughts. Focus on more rational explanations.
3. Practice your slow, gentle breathing.
4. Expect some anxiety and use your coping techniques.
5. Focus on what's really happening to you and around you — not what you fear might happen.
6. Wait for your fear to decrease and notice when it begins to fade. If you leave, return as soon as possible to continue practice!
7. Each practice situation is an opportunity for progress.
8. Celebrate your successes no matter how small. They will add up!

FIRST ALERT CARD

FIRST ALERT CARD

About the Authors

Shirley Babior, LCSW, MFCC, is a psychotherapist in private practice in San Diego, California, and co-director of the Center for Anxiety and Stress Treatment. Previously she resided in Boston, Massachusetts, where she helped found the Greater Boston Phobia Society, of which she was vice president. She has lectured on the treatment of anxiety disorders at numerous professional meetings and adult education workshops. Shirley is a former regional governor of the Phobia Society of America and board member of the Society of Behavioral Medicine.

Carol Goldman, LICSW, was director of Behavior Associates from 1977 to 1989. She is a founding director of the Boston Institute of Cognitive-Behavior Therapies, a training program for mental health professionals. As the past president of the Greater Boston Phobia Society, Carol worked with professionals and anxiety sufferers to increase public awareness about anxiety disorders. Carol is currently in private practice and specializes in cognitive-behavior therapy, family systems, and couples therapy.